1960

MOMENT IN OSTIA

By Sister M. Thérèse

Poetry

NOW THERE IS BEAUTY
GIVE JOAN A SWORD

Anthology

I SING OF A MAIDEN

MOMENT IN OSTIA

SISTER M. THÉRÈSE

Hanover House
Garden City, New York
1959

Library of Congress Catalog Card Number 59-6376
Copyright © 1957, 1958, 1959 by Doubleday & Company, Inc.
Printed in the United States of America
First Edition

ACKNOWLEDGMENT

The Author and the Publisher are most grateful to the following magazines, newspapers and publishers, for permission to include in this volume the poems mentioned below:

America Press for DE ANGELIS.
The Commonweal for LADY OF THE GENESEE and RARE IS THIS GIFTING.
Knock Shrine Society (Ireland) for CNOC MHUIRE.
Liveright Publishing Company for THE BIRD and THE TRAVELER.
Loras College (Dubuque, Iowa) for THE CHIPMUNK and ROOF-TOP.
The Magnificat (Manchester, N.H.) for CALLING ALL SINGERS.
The *New York Herald Tribune* for AGAINST THIS WIND.
The *New York Times* for ON RE-READING A LETTER and WITH THIS SMALL KEY.
Sesame for ONE WHO SPOKE LIGHTLY OF DEATH.
The Sign for QUO VADIS.
Spirit for THE WREN, HOUSES, OUT OF MY POVERTY, and TROUBADOUR.
Thought for MOMENT IN OSTIA.
Wings for TO JOAN OF ARC ON D-DAY.

TO C.H.H.

with gratitude

Dedit ei Dominus sapientiam
et prudentiam multam nimis:
et latitudinem cordis, quasi
arenam, quae est in littore maris.

3 KINGS 4:29

CONTENTS

Page

ONE EXISTENTIAL MOMENT

Moment in Ostia   11
Journey into Light   13
A Question of Theology   15
Roof-Top   17
The Chipmunk   19
The Wren   21
Marriage in Malta   23

PHILOSOPHERS, BREAK YOUR KEYS

The Christus   27
Testament   29
De Angelis   31
The Lotus Flower   33
For Simone Weil   35
For One Who Spoke Lightly of Death   37
Calling All Singers   39

OF HER OWN PATRIMONY

Cnoc Mhuire   43
Knock Revisited   45
To No One Other   47
Lady of the Genesee   49
For Neva   50
In Genazzano   52

IN THE STRAITS OF SILENCE

Rood-Flower   57
Scenario   59
Houses   61

7

	Page
Portrait	63
The Contemplative	65
Monastery Detail	66

OUT OF GOD'S TREE

Rare Is This Gifting	71
Atlantis	73
Ballad of the Calla Lily	75
Junior Dialectic	77
Interrogative	79
Out of My Poverty	80
Troubadour	82

JOAN, BE SWIFT

To Joan of Arc on D-Day	85
Spring—1944	86
Quo Vadis	87
At the Third Milestone	88
Operation Bethlehem—1952	89

IN SYMBOL AND ANALOGY

Bright Stranger	93
On Re-reading a Letter	93
The Bird	94
The Traveler	94
Against This Wind	95
Talisman	95
With This Small Key	96

ONE EXISTENTIAL MOMENT

MOMENT IN OSTIA
(St. Augustine, *Confessions,* ix, 10, 23–26)

Spliced between Milan and Carthage this strip of days
In the port city, while the heart recruits
Quiet, aware that the trim ship tethered
At dockside crouches mad to spring
The foaming jungles to the tropic shore.

But where is argument for rest
When the precipitate spirit flays
Her wings in the sealed cage?

Unless that conjuring sirocco
That blows the window full of stars
Where Monica and Augustine lean into the night
Shall crack the aviary—

Parrying speech like lances
The birds escape and jet
Past moon and sun and every constellation,
The pedantry of matter, the linear plateaus
Of syllogism, the blaze of the analogies—
Out-distancing Plotinus infinitely—
Till with a last fine thrust of heart
They touch a little on that timeless moment
That lets them into Wisdom,
Beneath whose molten, syllableless text
The *Enneads* are ice.

An instant only—
Life in this stratosphere is execution
For birds still trapped in matter;
Lest sinew snap, bone melt, and blood unchannel
Love tricks them back into their hapless cages.

The night drops strict enclosure,
Leaving of this sharp flight

One visible sign:
A tired woman leaning on the sill,
Her son beside her watching the starlight sing
On the garden stones, loud as the light that played
Across his intellect, making new parables
Of the past months' presents:
A childvoice rising in a trifling rhyme;
The tears, the book, the stabbing word,
The irresolute resolution;
Monica wrestling with God till past her prayer
The invincible lightnings struck
The wincing cauldrons of Carthage to sifted snow,
The lions of Tagaste to their knees in the African sand.

i

All journeys of a lifetime might have led
To this one terminal;
All moments might have melted into this
One existential moment, beautiful
As a phrase of Mozart staffed on naked light—
When in the first wind of surprise
I stood marvelously quickened
By the smile of your eyes,
The swift joy of your hand.
Nothing of time and space
Marred our encounter on this perfect day;
Our only witness in this place:
A crossroad lying clean and bright
As truth in the intellect,
And four fields of summer
Golden and circumspect.

ii

We took an evening road
Of sculptured clarity,
Whose detail I had never seen
Were it paved with porphyry,
For the cloud that wrapped me held my sight
Blind to the finite hour:
My only light—your presence
That opened like a flower;
My only sound—your silence
I could touch and be not afraid,
For closer than any melody
Was the hush your spirit made;
Though each young daisy at the hedge
Was singing like a bride,
Yet I heard no music
But the music at my side—
A sharp, running gladness
Along the blood blown
Of iris chanting in your flesh,

And lilies singing in the bone;
A road spinning to darkness,
Far lights of a little town,
You of the Christ-look, radiant,
As all the stars leaned down.

iii

On brief maps of a lifetime one may chart
His journeys one by one,
And find where he has ended
There he has begun—
When in one miraculous moment
Without plan or plot,
Spirit speaks to spirit
What the heart cannot.
Always I feared the wisdom
Shining in your face
Structured of austere beauty,
Disciplined by grace,
Yet I brought you my thoughts unsorted,
Rolling my hoops of words
Over your narrow threshold
To rest, like tired birds,
Till warmed by your compassion,
And new-winged in the bright
Tents of your mind, you loosed them
For their journey into light.

iv

Though skies be plumed with terror
The spirit will find a way
If love will drop but one feather
To tell its flight. From this day
No more shall I move lonely
Or lightless through the dark,
Remembering these fields, this crossroad,
And the commentary of the lark;
With one beloved standing
As you stood the days before—
Like April thunder at my window,
And like the morning star in my door.

A Weimaraner and black Labrador
Anticipant, leap to the door,
Retrieving us from the night,
Then with a light
Gesture of informality
Take over all the subtler points
Of hospitality
And constitute themselves
Hosts for the evening.
They supervise the smörgåsbord
Meticulously
Lest any crumb be lost;
Then nuzzle us into chair and divan where
As a most wondering audience
We view their lightsome capering,
Till at the apex of their play,
Tiring of quick response
To human idiom,
They sink to quiet on the rug
And gaze on us contemplatively
Without a move or sound,
Making it easy to surmise
How when the trees unleaf in November weather,
They might cradle a bird in their soft mouths
And never break a feather.

Yet their tense look disturbs me.

What do they search for in our faces?
As if they sensed some shining thing
Gladder than sun on a bird's wing
That wakes a reminiscence
Of that bright day in Genesis
When in a percept unforgotten
They touched the splendor
Of hands that fashioned them;
And we, close-creatured in that image,
Recall that moment fleetingly.

Wherefore this terrible watching
At the dark crevices of our being
For one swift sight
Of that pristine light?

But better skilled in these elate
Matters, let theologians speculate.

Meanwhile I shall content myself with this
Simpler hypothesis:
Might they not see
Clairvoyantly
The day of the last hunt when their good master
After a lifetime of seeking shall bag his quarry
And rapturously gather God
From the last thickets of this darkling world—
Then like a rocket hurled
They will streak past him to the gate of stars
To shout his coming at that joyous place;
Even as Scripture tells the delightful story
How one of their ancestral kin
Troubled the heels of an angel long ago
On the perilous journey to Rages and return,
And though
In deference to heaven's wish the angel led—
On the last stretch of hillside nearing home
Tobias' little dog ran on ahead.

Two dragon-flies dispute my presence here
Above this city set like a Cézanne
Complete with mountain back-drop,
But I have learned to disregard
The hot blue motors in their wings
And shadows on my Scripture—
For I can close the book and savor silence
With God in the wind. Till on a day,
From nowhere, like a fear, a bird flew up,
Alit, and stood his distance fluttering.

Now in my categories
Of meager knowledges birdlore is imprecise,
Though I would recognize
Lanier's marsh hen or Eliot's hermit thrush
At nest on the printed page;
But not this species, living, nondescript,
On a bleak roof-top.

From out my ignorance
I took it for a fledgling, its swift panic
A hunger cry, so for the piteous starveling
I ran for food and water.
But the bird frightened, flew into the trees.

At dusk, by woman's more than intuition
I climbed the height to see
If by some homing instinct it had come
Back to my compassion;
I sought the corner softly, with new caution
Half hope, half fear
Lest I meet emptiness;
Still as the doves in the Hadrian mosaic
There sat my grey contemplative
In its stark prayer-stall on the scattered stones
Lost in some wonder I might never guess,
Or some deliberate intent
To prove to me
In its small universe it was entirely competent.

I pitied it until it flew—
Then in a flash I knew
What this bright vigil hermit-like was for:
Two mottled eggs lay on the bare floor.

One comes to wisdom variously
In small and simple places
Where mystery nests beside one unobserved;
Even a hawk solemn and sinister
Carries some wild flame in her breast
To kindle knowledges one will not find
Beneath the scholar's dome or minaret;
And one learns more than Scripture walking with God
Upon this parapet.

Opon the ledge beside the tennis court
I lay my books and sundry magazines
To walk in solitude
Pondering the essences of things:
How love pervades the universe—
And I am taken by the gravity
Of a dissertation on *Eros* and *Agape*
Wherein some scholar happily reconciles
What from the first was never disparate;
Or a comment on Ortego's humanism,
Of God a 'constant' in all our perspectives.
Trapped on the edge of insight
One brooks no interruption.

When suddenly along the fence
A small grey lightning—
He is there!
Half Pavlova half quicksilver,
Sniffing at all my precious things
The wind has wide disheveled:
Atlantic, Blackfriars take his pirouettes;
Flipping *SR* with an arabesque
He dances down Eliot's *Four Quartets;*
Then giving *Renascence* a critical glance
He catapults to *Jubilee* blown wide
At a child's cut-outs done from Noah's ark,
As if to comment marginally
That this at least makes sense.
One foot shifts delicately on a page
Of Simone Weil as if it touched a star—
And having surveyed cursorily
My enthusiasms as they are,
He settles motionless on the eminence
Of Merton's *Mountain*
To regard me quizzically
With an arch look that would deflate
A reader most discriminate.

I wince before his glance
Who would not trade his instinct knowledges
For all my world of syllogisms.

But piqued, and swift to my defense
I would point up an ignorance
To flutter the complacency
Of this small philosopher—
No sharpest wisdom from his cosmic store
Would ever lead him to suspect
That recklessly he is confronting
With such high scorn the secondary causality
That daily, deliberately,
Places that brown nut at his little door.

The day was spring and all your smiling hedges
Celled us apart
Sun-cloaked against the multiplicity
That trafficks in the heart
To set us free within this perfect garden—
Where at the green-spired apple with your wish
Scarce uttered that the birds would come
To summer in your tree, the brown wings fell
In a swift furrow flung
Obliquely where the swinging hospice hung;
And even as we gazed the young wren stood
On its small threshold tentatively
Tilted against the wind, his being caught
And joyed in this pendant vision,
While a summer of birdsong waited tremblingly
On his brief decision.

Swift his assent—the delicate balance-wheel
Of his small choices circled and was still:
Weighed and found wanting was each sunny sill
Of cloud matched with your tree's still grace,
The wide halls of the sky with this small singing place,
Covers of thunder and of sun
With this dark bough where frightened birds might run—
Surer than any silver dialectic
His flawless intuition
That told him this was very joy
By any definition.

Yet swifter than the wren and his felicitous choosing
Was the instant, blessed bruising
Of heart stretched to new wisdom as we knew
No casual thrust of wind or word
Brightened your branches with this bird.

And I, the guest you brought into your garden
Stood wonderingly
That your slightest wish should be a swift command
To him who holds all birds in his hand;

And the little leaves broke into infinite conversation
Knowing the secret sign
On the lilac, grass and clover
That the granaries of his love are running over
Who beautifully scatters
Wrens into trees to gladden his elect
Who labor in the gardens of the spirit
Pruning the branches of the intellect
To a spare brightness that new truth may bloom;
Who in the gloom
Of the sharp deserts of the double night
Bending above the furrows of the will
Seeds the quick heart with light;
And the leaves called out to each other that it was He
Whose glory blinds to darkness the sun's bright lens
That had left his wind of joy blow through your garden,
Kindled your tree with wrens.

MARRIAGE IN MALTA

(For Dr. John Pick and Marchesa
Cecilia Barbaro of St. George)

This April in Malta
Let the bells beat
And fortune favor
Each fishing fleet.

Lids of Osiris
Lift with surprise
As the two lovers
Miracle-wise

Here at Valetta's
Sea-locked door,
Find what their hearts
Are seeking for.

Precious as platinum
Carried from far,
Or a multitude
Of rubies are,

Or wisdom the scholar's
Diadem—
Love infinitely
Surpasses them.

Though human weal
Be blent with rue,
Nothing but joy
Dare touch these two

Who, sweetly wound
In bands of grace
Seal their troth
In this ancient place.

The fish, their love's
High symboling,
Is *Ichthus,* Christ,
Their marriage ring.

Then scatter the wheat
And the ripest grain
Over their heads
In a holy rain.

While skies of Malta
With bright wings move—
God's son and daughter
Plight their love.

PHILOSOPHERS, BREAK YOUR KEYS

THE CHRISTUS

(On a gouache by John Pick)

Philosophers, break your keys, there is no lock
To this high door; this delicate winding wall
Is steel to the cool shafts
Of intellection; let the taut reins fall;
Your keenest coulters cut only the dawn
Between the cobblestones of sense,
But where the intense
Blazing afternoon settles and the wind is wine
You skirt only the lowest timberline
Of peaks divinely wooded,
For where the everlasting cedars lift their heads and cry,
Even metaphysics must go discalced and hooded.

Beneath the artist's brush
The opaque pigment is diaphanous
With the naked light
That sang through him like music searching to name
Its three-syllabled flame
In the sharp delight
Of image seared in the crucibles of art—
The presence printed on the heart
No artist can define
Save in stark symmetry of form and line:
Here is the measureless
Measured, the boundless set in space
Of our dimensions, the white eternities
Caught in our nets of color, the nets of love,
Till nerve and sinew, flesh and bone
Livingly glow
In the alone
Anointed not with oil but Godhead
Whose gentle Face
That looked at Peter at cock-crow still prays the night

Endlessly at the olive with whatever man
Shall know Him, with soul whipped clean, and heart torn
By the invisible thorn;
Here is the tenderness that lights the promised city,
The sorrow and the pity
Quick with the love that escapes all category,
Incarnate in a story
That wears no legend but that by which the heart is stirred
When all its wildernesses are broken
By a Word.

Upon what rock was dreamed this dream?
From out what singing deserts sounded the delicate flute
That waked the artist to arise and scatter
The exigencies of matter
And flood his canvas with the absolute?
On this steep terrain human words are thinned,
And questions blow like thistles in the wind—

You must come up from all the little valleys
And tent here at the cedars where the air
Is limpid silence everywhere;
Having passed by the little inns of speaking, hearing, seeing,
Enter the inner country of your being;
In its most hidden place
Kneel where the artist knelt, with him discover
The secret of that Face!
Held by its beauty, strength, and power
Gather your answer in this hour
Effortlessly, as a child would pluck a flower;
Lay by the careful industry of keys,
No longer need they trouble lock or bar,
For reason hides her inadequate lamp beneath her mantle
When all the night is a star.

TESTAMENT

(In memory of my father)

His hands worked ceaselessly at the coverlet
Folding and smoothing it again
In that hushed interval between living and dying.
A craftsman's hands, firm knit and sinewy,
That for a lifetime span
Busied with brush and pigment
Disciplined neutral surfaces
To beauty's clarity and proportion.
Now in this time of unaccustomed quiet
Come upon them so suddenly
They wrestle with the idle moment
Urgent to execute
Some artifact to dictates of the mind
That is now moving into a new pattern,
And the sole industry of contemplation.

Since that first precept given in Paradise,
Yaweh to Adam—keep and dress the land—
Work is a blessed thing.
Even after trespass and the shut gate
Labor is holy—
Not *sui generis* a slavery,
But sign of the liberty of the sons of God;
A dialogue with Him in His creation
Who, by a unique ordering
So fashioned man an intellectual being
Whose singular delight would be
To conspire with Him to help each creature
Attain its end the more abundantly.
Thus the more praised is God.

In the sublime chironomy of toil,
This collusion between creator and his creature,
Hands execute the ineffable purposes,
Make corporate the existential spark
That glows like a Pleiad in the creative mind:
Adam our father, working the recalcitrant glebe
Into soft furrows, the Etruscan's dream

Caught in the fragile vase, the medieval soul
Leaping in Chartres.
Rodin, Rouault, Auden, Prokofiev—
Like a little white cloud a concerto springs from the ivory;
And a canticle from the rock of Morningside.

Still, in the execution
The ultimate focus is not upon doing but being;
As in God's cry in *Exodus* to build a tabernacle,
And in shaping of the cosmic habitation
Is builded the great temple of the spirit,
Rarer than shittim wood and onyx stone,
Over which the *Shekinah* shall more than brood,
But live as in His own house.

My father's work is done.
His simple testament
I can well ponder all my days:
Witness by these presents
Of hands so bent on the divine routine
In their long dialogue with reality
That they refuse to rest
Even as the last darkness gathers in,
And the spirit entering a new dimension
Has left them orphans.
For man the maker lives in no cactus land;
His hands are not impersonal,
But keep the gladdening rhythms of toil
Even as God's hand closes over them
And the great door of death swings sharply
Into the endless Sabbath.
There is no opposition between work and contemplation,
In the sweat of his brow man lives and loves and sings
His ultimate hymn to God.

DE ANGELIS

(For C.P.D. who asked me to write about angels)

You asked me to write of angels—
But I can tell only of what I have seen,
Heard, touched, and loved.
I search my Aristotle
And find a first entelechy; in Aquinas
Dazzling intelligences, ungarmented
By the dear, perilous body
Even a God was partial to
And wore felicitously.
In Scripture we are told
That angels walked with men familiarly,
Even perchance made bold
By the celestial loan
Of some eidetic flesh they could not own,
Have eaten at our board
Brought little human messages,
Rebukes, companioning,
And disciplined Adam with a flaming sword.

But I am more at home
In other climates and terrain,
And better knowledged in that startling species
Of flesh and spirit
Poised on our human plane
Where there are mortals who,
Like you,
Standing so simply in my door,
Are a little less than the angels, and yet more—
Because of a mystic mark you wear
No multitude of waters can erase.
I see it in your face
Like an Angelico seraph, and in your voice
That kindles like a prayer.
When in the stress of a dark day
I see you standing there—
With an élan, a lightness

I lift my head to catch your brightness,
Remembering
That as a small child I was told
If ever I should meet
An angel or archangel on the street
With one like you beside him, never to forget
This point of theological etiquette—
Whom first to greet.
And though the words were told me long ago,
I still would know,
Nor even for an instant hesitate—
But give you my smile, my greeting, and my hand,
And let the angel wait.

THE LOTUS FLOWER

(A lotus seed discovered in a neolithic canoe
buried deep in a peat bog near Tokyo, blooms after
two thousand years.)

Enchanted flower
Centuries you slept
In your ancient cradle
And gravely kept

In the Stygian dark
Of the deep mire,
Your quintessential
Latent fire—

Quick with the hope
Of derelict things
Under residual
Blanketings

That a hand will touch them
Out of dream
Into awakeness,
And redeem

The sterile time
In the folded husk,
By a thrust of petals
Hung with musk.

You cast no lotus spell
Over men—
In four swift days
You slept again—

But stung him with transience
Of all dear things:
Broken petals
Like fallen wings;

Shook him with beauty
The one, the true,
The ever ancient,
The ever new.

Whose infinite caring
Is not star-crossed;
No seed is forgotten,
No love is lost.

But quickened by Wisdom
Will rise like a bride
On that *ultima Thule*
Where all boats are tied.

FOR SIMONE WEIL

As a shy deer that hurtles into sunlight
From some dark covert, unswervingly
Your being leaped to truth.
Mystic, philosopher, who lived on summits
That brush God's sill
Where nests that brilliant bird that sings
In the bone-caged spirit
When every other bird is still.

Upon your spare, translucent page
Your mind lies luminous as God made it;
Even the heart scooped hollow as a gourd
Comes upon opal-fire
Among the branches of your thought,
Lighting it back to wisdom;
And the most laggard comer
May reap of leaf and bud and flower
An intellectual summer.

Clean of all sophistry
You had no fear of the dark wood,
You had no dreams to break
Who coveted but to take
Your place among the poor who wrest their bread
From the gaunt furrow and their cup of water
From the split rock overhead.

Then share one bright immortal moment
With us who grope in this lost Eden
Frightened and alone—
Show us again that when one asks for bread
God will not give a stone;
We who have seen our fairest justices
Lie as a broken toy in a child's hand,
Seek a word, a face, a season
That will transmute the whole,
When the blessed slavery of affliction
Loses one half his soul.

Then fix our eyes upon that dazzling point
Your philosophers dared not see,
Where creator and creation intersect
At the cross-branched tree;
Quicken our feet upon the stair you took
Past reason's naked rafter
As you stumbled toward the last long certitude—
Neither before nor after
Did your rich heart know loss;
If you stopped short of thresholds, did it matter,
If Love leaned down and lifted you across?

You shall not be pilloried for your remark
That rocked the class-room quiet,
Nor pressed in private for an exegesis,
Though hands are thickets in the air before me
As questions sharpen in the mind
To war against your words.
With one terse comment I shall blunt their spears
And hush the attack.

It is no time for reprimand or question—
Your face is clean of any hurt
To heart or doctrine
Of those who have so tightly set their stakes
In groove of definition
They cannot move their tents to higher places
Where love may run untethered in the wind;
The varied songs we learned by rote,
The stereotyped response,
Deaden the finer silences
Where the volatile air hangs hot
With incandescent fire.

Could we but read the spirit,
Might you not blind us by the shining
Of that indefinable essence
That plants theology in the mind's quick substance?

My heart shall merely counsel and say go,
Anima naturaliter Christiana,
Blithely in the innocence of your singing
Along the worn paths of the academe;
Loiter with Plato and with Aristotle
Whose texts you feed on;
Love your immutable sea;
Till some quick morning off your starboard bow
Truth will come walking toward you on the water
Striking a flame from every crest;
And you will steer for shore, no more the searcher,
Or voyager, but the pursued, the taken;

A new Ulysses you will hurry back
To tell us of the wonder—
Dazzle our minds with startling narrative
Of some new star you gazed on brighter than Vega,
Of feet you heard walking the wild night sea.

Homer from out his blindness wrought a song
Untouched by time, unbarriered by space—
Still with immortal grace
Her fingers hot against a raveled blur,
Penelope leaves her loom and scans the night
For one white star to comfort her;
While on the wine-dark deep
Odysseus searches under sun-scorched hand
For lost hills on the sky.
Mute at the Skaian gates the Elders stand
As Helen passes by.

Up from the catacombs' thick dark
Is rumor of a lark—
A young girl stirs in her gold brocade
And luminous is the note
From triple wounded throat.

Above the smoke and faggots piled
Beyond all human pity,
The maid Joan smiled
At a voice within her—a child could hear it
Above the searing of her spirit—
Out of essential joy it came,
Out of the many furrowed flame,
The deathless Name.

Juan from his prison wove his canticle
Of dark nights rich and full
Whose gloom is brightness as the noonday sun,
Charting for those who run
The rugged contours of the mystic mountain
A pathway sure and strait;
And still the poor, the desolate
Feel a new springtime in their blood, and free
Run rapturously
The road of quiet where all turnings bend
To the secret fountain
Where all roads end.

On grim Salerno's beaches where the tide
Lapped crimson, impotent to hide
Travail of sharp, hot rain,
Singers have lain
Who made a psalm of pain;
For sharper than any steel God's finger pressed
With an immortal smart,
Working a delicate wonder of the heart;
While angels lifted from that bitter bar
Souls tempered to a star.

Since out of darkness, out of pain and wrong
Is precedence for song—
Lean to the Voice above all human voices
Calling all singers to unloose the birds
That sing in the heart, and let them soar and trace
Bright rhythms of words
Of that felicitous utterance which is grace;
Quicken the spent soul starting
At some new grief;
Make a sweet cry
Of the sharp, breathless parting,
And all men sorrow by;
Prepare the heart to brave the little shock
That lifts the spirit to a lyric shape;
Drain golden vintage from the bitter grape,
And honey from the rock!

OF HER OWN PATRIMONY

Our Lady has her choice of sanctuary—
Over the world she moved like folded light
Drawn to some luminous focus
Till the intricate coasts of Eire were at her feet,
When the little sea-winds that had run on before her
Turned inland suddenly
To a hamlet on the Mayo plain,
Whose huddled houses wept in the August rain.

Her love was punctual. Swiftly she came
To these the children of her predilection
In the late dusk of their most bitter dolor—
Quick as a mother starts—
To listen at their hearts;
To look to heaven in a wordless prayer
Mirroring back to God the light she had seen
Where faith flamed stark and pure;
Christ in the eyes,
Christ in the tired faces of the poor.

Mist did not blur her beauty nor the wind
Shatter her stillness as she stood
Two white suspended hours
With Joseph, John, the altar and the Lamb
Set at the cross beneath whose wood
She fruited in a mystic motherhood,
As swift as meadow flowers
Her children sprang up round her in the rain,
With never a doubt that it was she—
For if the star blossomed over a stable,
Might not the Mystic Rose
Bloom at a lonely gable?

This night of Knock will never have an ending:
She is here in the air, the wind, the fields, the sky;

Having no season other than compassion
No weather is she guided by
But the stricken soul's most desperate need,
Or a small child's lifted cry.

Who would discover her within this place
Where the fertile dust at her feet springs miracles,
Must warn his heart against the shock
Of new flesh flowering on the withered bone,
Or rivers singing from the rock,
As she leans and reaches her hand to the most forsaken,
While the stars sing at her gable here at Knock.

You did not ask a miracle
The day you came to her
Nailed to your cross—
But in some heavenly dimension
Where gain is loss
You let her love move as it would;
Whatever peace her hand might fashion
You would find good.

Nor did you ask her to come down
To loose you from the rigid tree;
Yours was a cry a saint might make—
Solely for love's sake—
Of total conformation to its wood;
And though she leashed the moment
To snatch you from pain,
A star stood where her hand had lain.

Your lips were still as mirrors
Holding the windless country of her eyes,
Your plea a petal floating
On the cool lake of her will,
As she searched your soul and found it beautiful.
Then in the wordless dialogue between you
She shaped a seven-year world
To day and hour when
On sky-keeled caravel
Swift as the wings of Gabriel
You would come back to her
From the heart's winter lands—
Light circling your face,
Chrism on your hands.

As she looks down today
On your new-sinewed strength
Splendidly whole
In perfect body matched to perfect soul—
Her thoughts are simple ones:

Remarking as a mother would
With proud felicity,
How you move, graced as she;
Or with a glad surprise,
How her smile plays in your eyes
As eloquent you stand
A witness to her love
In Knock her little town,
Like an archangel flashing
At the brink of heaven,
Whose words are bright larks flying down.

TO NO ONE OTHER

(With a picture of Christ in Gethsemani)

To no one other could I send
This poignant chronicle—
Fearing they would not comprehend
The more than mortal shock
Of Man broken against a rock
By terror and the stir
Of pain the ravager,
Seeing within the sky
The tree to hang him by.
But you who thrice have lain
Crushed beside him there
When every syllable is pain,
Would never be perplexed
Nor need to search a text
To pierce the gain-in-loss
Mystery of the cross;
For by that undimensional
Knowledge connatural
That is the subtle clue
To all the light of you—
You know it as your own
Defined in blood and bone—
Know as no other knows,
Touch as no other can
This worm and no man.

If I know aught of you,
This, I must truly know:
In that moon-fractured shade
Waited Knock's lovely maid
Lest you be pressed too far—
Those were His wounds you wore!
She leaned above their fire,
Like hurt birds lifted them
Out of the wind's rough hem,
Plucked them as roses torn

By too near touch of thorn
And set them delicately
Within her heart that day
To keep, or give away.

Since that most gracious hour
She wears you like a flower,
She sings you like a psalm;
And should your acres mourn
When night drops starkly bare,
And no words make a prayer,
Till the naked spirit flees
Alone to the olive trees—
Lest you be comfortless
All of her tenderness
Waits in the darkness there,
And though the stones be red
Lets light smile round your head.

The moated hills monastically close in
This gracious valley of her smile
Who planted here of her own patrimony
Long tents of peace along one quiet
Miraculous mile.

Where light hooves rang along the Genesee
Hot to the hunt, the hounds racing the wind,
Toward a new quarry fleeter riders run
Vaulting the thickets of midnight
With the flash of an antiphon.

The feathered-in-white-wool monks, the falcon-hooded,
Unjessed from Love's light wrist arrow to sky,
Then gyre into the fiery cloud
Of darkness, held and caught
By the prey they sought.

Before the face discovered in these faces
The mountains bow their heads—
All the ineluctable glories
Of Sion and Carmel
Lie crushed in these sheds.

Whosoever shall come into this valley—
Silence shall take him like a sea
In which his ruins drown,
Till the clean spirit rises luminously
As the great gull rushes down.

Tumult of town and porcelain laughter of city
Reach to this valley for their quieting
Where peace unfolds like psalms in the still night,
As the sweet chant unravels
And the young monks sing.

For these new tents of prayer stretched in the sun
Of the Empire State whose tilted hills enclose
Bright Bernard's progeny—
Above La Ferté, Rievaulx, Melleray,
Be loved, Lady, for the Genesee.

Not for the maiden of the fairy tale
Are you called Snow-white,
Though for your quiet loveliness
Well might some modern Cyrano
Sweep the broad pavement with his plume:
But so to guess at what might be
One of God's gayest secrets,
I shall not presume.

For you, with winsome mind troubled for truth
Through every veining of your being's root—
Yet with a spirit still a bit untamed
In its pursuit—
Are most felicitously named
For a fair Lady who once had her way
By a mere heavenly whimsy.
What if it were mid-summertime
In Latium?—a bright rectangle of snow
Geometrically precise, would show
Specific boundaries that all might see
Her exclusive property
Where on an August day peremptorily she chose
That they should build for her
Her chapel of the snows.

So patroned you are well forgiven
What the staid mind might label wild,
Presumptuous fantasy—
That one so wisely and demurely grown
Remembering she is still God's child
May reach for anything on His lavish table
And call it her very own.
Though there be margin for a Trappist fast,
Your ascesis wears another cast,
Your joy a sterner yoke—
Love is a hairshirt you cannot escape,
Loneliness fits you like a cloak;
Nor for celestial fashioning

Need you rent a desert cell—
Clutching God's hand you can find
Heaven on a carousel.

And it is meet that there are many mansions
In that house hung with sky—
You of the merry heart would never fit
The strictly chiseled stalls
Where the sombre-hooded sit—
If any saint be so, but I would argue it—
Still be not swift toward that apocalypse,
Nor let your Cyrano come too soon;

Stay yet a little at my side like spring
That with one sentient syllable
Sets the mind blossoming.
Scatter your words like bellsong
Out of tall turrets when we pause to play
Our little game of sparring text with text
Like glancing scimitars;
But when the perplexed
Spirit in the long night cries softly
Lest it waken the angels or perturb the stars—
Knock at her window in the sky
Whose name we call you by;
Have her look down a little on our woes
And succor us,
Your Lady of the Snows.

IN GENAZZANO
(After the landings at Anzio)

In 1461 a picture of the Madonna is said to have
been miraculously transported in a cloud from Scutari,
Albania, to Genazzano in the mountains near Rome,
leading the way to safety for two clients who had
asked the Virgin's help in fleeing from the Turks.
The picture is still preserved at Genazzano, and
venerated under the title, *Madonna del Buon Con-
siglio* Lady of Good Counsel.

In Genazzano
When nights are wild
Closer the Virgin
Holds her child

Who through the centuries
Leans questioning,
Asking of wisdom,
Some pitiful thing.

Lady, who stoops to
The least word we say,
Be pleased to answer
Your child today.

Why do the bright keels
Brush the sea-floor?
Angels of mercy
Come to our shore.

Why do the pines sob
In measured mode?
There are strange armies
Tramping the road.

Why do grey gulls drop
Fire from the sky?
God works His willing
In things that fly.

If on the mountain
Death lays his shroud?
I still shall lead them
Under a cloud.

Should the caves darken
Where strong men are?
I shall in heaven
Hang out a star.

Is there no answer
To this sharp woe?
God has His secrets
We cannot know.

But if their spears break
On gates of hell?
All will be well, and
All will be well.

IN THE STRAITS OF SILENCE

ROOD-FLOWER

Lines with a relic of the True Cross

(For Thomas Merton)

This is the amulet you diced for
On the top of your mountain, minstrel, and the odds
Were yours as you tossed the last bright coin of your life
Into the jar of silence, and the lid
Clamped on its beauty, shutting from us forever
The face God smiled on with a predilection.

Before the launching of the morning stars
Your name was cut
Into this fragment of the blessed tree;
Before the sentried seas rushed to their stations
Its branches yearned to you for their completing—
Till tensile time was pulled into this moment
That overtakes you as you come
Fresh from your Christ, sealed with a new sealing,
Your hands still running with the damp of olive.

Rehearse the piercing canticle you sang
Closing your history, where the neumes rise
Sheer on the staves of darkness,
Against whose argument
Your lovers have thrust their arrowy questionings.

But you, the initiate, laugh at the incongruity
Of their untutored fears, knowing the secret word
No other man has heard
Of seeds sown in the arid solitudes,
And a tree stark-timbered as a tower,
That waits new leafing and its newest flower.

Hang on it, minstrel, spike your limbs to its wood,
Its shaft to your heart

Where pain breaks and splinters like a shattered sun
And the songs start;
Stretch to its cross-beam, blossom along its length,
Rare rood-flower, till the rising sap
Whirls through the circuit of the brittle branches—
The tragic multitudes that pressed with you
Into your speechless valley, and beg
Their life of your sweet death:
Feed them with springtime from your barren tables;
Light summer in their hearts in your chill watchings;
Winter them where the fires leap in your prayer;
And the flutes of the redemption move on endlessly into the distance
As this dry wood flowers again
With the bright bloom of your body
Slain with your Christ.

SCENARIO

This is a drama like no other
That clutters Broadway—you are the spectator
Smug in your box who startled comes to find
Himself an actor signed
With the protagonist, and unforeseen
You must play opposite him in every scene:

He is the subtle mercenary
That trips you in the Wall Street of your self-content,
Shuffles your careful coins and lets them drip like water
To the damp street, leaving you mendicant
On life's bleak corner begging an only penny
To pay your banishment.

Even in the porches where the planets shout
Approval of your vanities
This sly astronomer finds you out,
Snatches your instrument, upsets the code
Of your meticulous precisions,
Then leaning on the bar
Of finity swings to sharp focus on the darkness hung
With one admonishing star.

This icon-breaker blithely merry
Invades the inmost sanctuary
Where all your little idols smirk and smile;
Scatters the incense, pulls the tapers down,
With loaded whips drives out the barterers
That fatten on the circumstance,
Then cleaves the darkness with the first
Bright antiphon of your deliverance.

Before his stubborn frown
The walls of your Alcatraz crumble down
To the wild rock and tide;
He searches you out in your most secret cell
Where you are prisoned with your pride,
From his inexorable scrutiny
You turn and run to the jails of the night to hide.

The dramatic argument is grooved to this conclusion:
That however you may run, or hide, or blind you
In your tumultous need
Upon this stage in this mad century he should find you
Poised on the craters of your disillusion—
But just before the final curtain crashes
On the black plunge of despair
He is your brother waiting there
With all the quick solicitudes of love
To sweep you with him into the path
Of that imperious whirlwind which is the spirit blowing
Out of our frustrate world up the seven-circled mountain—
Where he shares with you a blessed bread
Baked in no earthly ovens, and the cool shock
Of water from the rock,
Then striking from your hand the wizened berry
Plucked on the shales of desolation,
He bids you taste the shining apples
That ripen on the tree of contemplation;
Nor does he leave you, starveling of the spirit,—
Your brother warm and winning—
Till he has seen you past the winter acres
Of pride and paltry sinning
And set you clean and shining in the sun
Splendidly, at your end and your beginning.

HOUSES

(St. Bernard speaks to a Trappist)

I am come down to Clairvaux—
Not that of Champagne where the arches sweeten
The valley of absinthe, but to this newer landscape
Where you are building in the living rock.
I bring this small stone from my ancient dwelling,
My own house made of flesh and bone
Through which the Spirit blew
A life-span through.

For in that unmoving interval when eternity and time
Are one, I heard you come
Over our mountains and beside our rivers,
Blithe traveler, and beyond my narrow window
I saw a light spread over all the countries
In a sharp snare
To trick your feet; then gathering all your trails
Tied them in one that blazed across the water,
Cut to mid-continent, and left you lost,
Blissfully lost within this holy valley.
Then I saw rising fleets of words
That flew across the world like birds.

Centuries unwind: I come to your low cave
Set in the slim fold of my Lady-house,
For I have heard your songs,
Watched you turn tenderly the brittle parchment
Searching the innermost valences
Of all my words
To brand them upon the lithe, the little cedars
That bend their fronds to touch this windless water.

Speech flies away; we sit and look at each other;
Love needs no word;
Dialectic is superfluous
Where all is bright conclusion.

Then build this little stone into the wall
Not of the corner or the tower
But in that delicate masonry
Shaped to hold fire
That races it meteors past its human borders.
Like-textured, it will fit without a seam
Against that desperate day
When Love shall make his last invasion.

When Satan's muscled might pounds at your gate
Laugh in your house, its locks are tight;
When the young foxes tunnel beneath your vines
Smile out your window, for they harry stone;
But when the tides of fire sweep in
That are both cautery and canticle
And there is no defense
Against the weight of God—
No little place to run and hide
For Love is everywhere—
When the gates crack and walls are hurled apart,
And the last familiar scaffold is become
A cross-beam for your crucifixion,
Then falter, if you must, against this stone
That knew light plight,
It will support and cover you
In the strict and naked night,
It will be music at your heart,
A Raphael sent
To succor you and bring you food and water
When all the substance of your house is spent.

PORTRAIT

... seek daily the faces of the saints.

(The Didache)

Posit no name or legend here
To clutter with peripheral knowledges
This presence blazing on my wall—
For having shrugged off premise and conclusion
And taken wisdom on
This metaphysics moves without comment
In the straits of silence felicitous as mountain water.

The accurate shutter fell on more than light and shadow
When the lens caught in its impersonal frame
This face of lustral quiet
Defenceless in its dazzling jail
Of fire flowering under the spare bone;
It cut to essences, leaving this chronicle
Of one who in a dark night went down
Into the thickets of unpossession
To keep the inexorable appointment
Wherein was struck from him
In one irrevocable exchange
All that he owned of self:
The delicate dream for discipline,
Crown for a thorn-branch and sharp scars;
Who coming up from that encounter
Clad only
In the borrowed being lent by love
Confronts us with this face of suns
That for all its careful custody
Shouts its secret
Of having late looked upon some burning bush,
Leaving to Sinai no monopoly of vision.
Citizen of two countries—earth and heaven—
He lightly walks their intersected rims
Gloriously free
Daring a stand on all our raucous corners
To hold bright conference with beggars and with kings,
While waiting by the shining waterfalls

Where all the air is a golden lark
As he talks in madrigals
To his only One
Who momentarily speaks and vanishes in a blue lunge of hills.

Metaphor cracks and spills its futile pictures
As sand, only the heart dare interpret
And leap to the solving
Though it break and be mended in one cry—
Seeing what love has done to all the windows
In this brief house of pilgrimage.

Who looks upon my wall dies to pretense,
Is scoured of plot and foil
And exorcised of uncompassion.
Stumble here in the dawn, the noon, the night,
Search out this grave-sweet face
Whose look needs no unriddling:
A stillness that cannot be broken,
A warmth that cannot be chilled
Of docile tissue and bone that have so completely taken
The print of love that it can break you with joy,
Or ply you with lashes to the bitter bone.
Let all your need kneel here,
Look up, and while the wonder grips you
Of God moving mysteriously in a human face,
Let the blue-dark tenderness of eyes—
Shorelights at last from your interminable Atlantics—
Point all your prows one way;
And while the transfigured lips
Bright as an Easter trope
Close yours on the unutterable Word
They feed on endlessly,
God pours in a hurricane through this paper portrait
To swamp your need and founder you
In the arms of his clean saint,
To be caught up, held, miraculously
Christed, that you forget
The lean loaf and the aloes-cup
For being healed and housed in infrustrable love.

He walks where clean lakes lie
At the mind's center; fleeing the laughter
Of gaudy Arab counters
He trades in marts of silence purchasing
With the sole coin of love,
Pity in baskets, peace in wineskins
For the starved prisoners at the broken gate.

His life is paradox.
Drained empty as the crumpled jugs that wait
At the forsaken cisterns,
He brims with the strange sweetness
Of dripping honeycomb that damps and cools
The spirit's caustic crust.

Distance is ridiculous; he takes the Atlantic
In prayer's bright syllable,
And owns the islands of the tropic seas;
Blinded to multitudes he sees each man
A Christ-face pleading toward him;
And he folds his brothers pitiful to his side
In one white pleat of his robe.

His prayer is inarticulate.
Words lost all pertinence and definition
As a secret, brilliant worm
That tunnels tracks of fire through all his being
Shatters the bright phrase like an ancient wall
Struck by a hurricane, and he is dumb
As one that stood on Pilate's polished stair.

Thus from the simple letter in my hand
I enter worlds of knowledge,
And learn of an industry that fills
Moment to moment endlessly,
For which one formula suffices:
A Word on the lips that never passes them,
And in the heart the total acquiescence
That softly, effortlessly
Slips the catch that opens the soul to love.

MONASTERY DETAIL

(Enter Saint Agnes with a basket of songs)

I carry these with me everywhere I go—
Dearer they are than any canticle;
When we crowd the porches to watch the planets play
The little saints have often questioned me
Of the songs that fly like thrushes round my hair;
And though you may have sent them yesterday—
Since love has neither ending nor beginning—
For centuries I have heard them in the wind
And knew the singer in the hooded sun
That walked to compline over Ostia;
We romped together in the saffron summers
When I caught white butterflies on the Nomentana.

You laughed with me when the gyves slipped from my hands
Too small for fetters, when the flames turned dew;
You wept with me from human tenderness
When my hair was shorn like lambs' wool in the spring;
That morning when I dressed for martyrdom
With a thrust of scarlet petals at my throat,
I touched your soul and found it kin to me:
Your robe as white as mine, of new lambs' wool,
Will take the Bosran dye (mine in one stroke),
Yours in the javelins of ten thousand days.

A man would not sing of a maid unless he loved her;
With only your songs for passport I came through
The willow sentries of your first frontier;
Finding no statute that would bar the coming
Of one who enters without mortal sound,
I did not trouble the gate, but came up softly
With the young lambs and stood at the outer door,
Till the Lamb that is lamp of my city let me in.

I shall perform the simple ministrations,
The little casual things a sister is for:
To take your hand when you wander in the hills,
Or run beside you along the enchanted stream

And show you things that only a child can see;
To sweep the vault and keep the tables neat
Where the young scholars come to raid the wisdoms
Locked in your heart and carry them away;
Or sit with you beneath the cedar trees
Listening to God in the long silences,
But most in your heart, my brother, my troubadour;
And perhaps within some withering night of spirit
I may hold the lamp and feed the little flame,
And warm you with my stillness and my love
Till manna falls into your parching hand,
And fountains leap up in the wilderness.

OUT OF GOD'S TREE

RARE IS THIS GIFTING

(For C.H.H.)

The Lord gave him wisdom and understanding exceeding much: and largeness of heart as the sand that is by the sea-shore.

(3 *Kings* 4:29)

As I walked in a far country
In the new clarity of dawn,
In a dream that was a strange waking
Suddenly I came upon
A stranger in whose brief greeting
Flashed some locked mystery,
As if an avalanche of stars were shaken down on him
Out of God's tree.

Plaited in the syllables of his conversation
Heard in the spirit, or not heard—
Was an experiential knowledge tasted only
In the tents of the Word;
Though in the dialectic of that sky
I am swift as a swallow,
The arrowing of his intellect toward truth
I could not follow,
Nor name the gentleness that spread
Across my wastrel lands
From his illimitable heart
Wide as the ocean sands.

Rare is this gifting and as rare
The encounter in this place.
Blinding the light I saw transfigure
His human face
When sharply hurled against the rood
His dreams thrice-crossed,

71

By cautery of wounds seared in the bone
He counted life well lost.

In my most towering need
I had not hoped to meet
One in whom love and wisdom
Were so complete
As to make of bleak rocks round him
A place of sapphires where
To mine Christ in caves of darkness
Down stark shafts of prayer.

How does one traffic with a mortal
So graced among men
That in his being splendorously
Both Bernard and Aquinas live again?
Is there no protocol?
In *Sirach* the answer soars—
Run to him early in the morning,
And wear down the steps of his doors!

This was an island set felicitously
In an alien sea.
Whenever my small boat touched its shore
Time dropped away and I ran
With the swift feet of a child
To a new identity.

The spread wings of your presence
Patterned a new dimension—
An ontological plenitude
Within whose orbit I have seen
How all of heaven can lean
Upon a man alone—
Until each perfect feature brightens
By a light that curves from some high secret place,
Signing beatitude
On a human face.

When April woke on our small island
Life sang in the leaf;
Lilies flashed up the hills like dancers
Sheaf on sheaf;
And like two children in a fairytale
We strolled along the morning of the world
A shining while in which you tutored me
In mysterious things,
And showed me the little hidden places
Where God sits and sings.

Whether we played together on the mountain
Watching the wild clouds soar,
Or sought the whorled shell on the windy shore,
Our dialectic wore no conversation
Other than silence;
The sheerest word was contraband
As star by star the night opened,
Even Orion blinded
By the light caught in your hand.

But seasons pivot without warning;
June is winter; my little boat is shoaled;
And though you went out singing,
The hermit's hut is isolate and cold.
And I would gather up my soul and flee forever—
Leaving Atlantis to the undersea,
Were I not circumscribed by your promise
Precious as the grail;
From the sweet south I have not missed a sail;
Knowing that in some unpredictable moment
Spring will return for a day
When with a rush of larks your voice is upon me,
And your love is a table spread
Where you reach me the cups of sun stored in your cellars,
And break me the stars for bread.

BALLAD OF THE CALLA LILY
(For Scottie)*

I came from Kenmare, Head of the Sea;
Though its misty surge break through
My song, it is no dreamer's ballad,
But true as love is true.

Years on years in a Kerry garden
By the church of the Holy Rood,
We watched the colleens as they passed
In lacy shawl and snood.

There came a maid from Coomnakilla
Who moved like a silver cloud,
She touched each white upswirling petal
As it slipped its emerald shroud.

Always she left her smile upon us,
And at the church a prayer;
Till one spring our garden woke to sadness,
She came no longer there.

The sea ran up the estuary
To tell us the bitter tale—
It had seen her last on those western waters
Where the tall ships sail.

Each shamrock, rose, and lily mourned her,
From the wild hills to the quay;
The years drew their veils more close about them
Till early one June day

From over the ocean there came a lady
Fair as the Kerry skies,
And I saw our maid of Coomnakilla
Shine in her daughter's eyes.

* Agnes Redmond Ziesler, daughter of Ella Brennan, "the maid of Coomnakilla."

The lady bent low in the Irish garden
Under a blur of tears,
She lifted my roots while yet my petals
Slept in their green spears.

We flew to the land of the west together
With the clouds for caravel;
I was her love in her dainty kitchen—
But I could not break the spell

That bound my leaf and sleeping flower
To my lovely lost Kenmare;
Mid-March was adrift, but how could I blossom
Under a foreign star?

But one swift dawn I heard a flutter
Of song in my lady's throat;
In its prisoning sheaf my unlocked petal
Stirred to the lilting note—

As I seemed to hear on a cobbled roadway
The Irish bagpipes play;
In an alien land I leaped to blossom
Upon St. Patrick's day!

For love is a country without borders—
It touches each uttermost land;
The wind, the skies, and the turbulent waters
All meet in God's hand.

And the eyes of this daughter of Coomnakilla
Shine like the Irish dew,
For she knows my song is no dreamer's ballad,
But true as love is true.

I walked into springtime
From the red-gold autumn hills
To hear truth leap like a young deer,
Wisdom ripple like rills
As girls pretty as young trees
Blossomed in argument:
Is love's bond forever?
Who could be indifferent?
But for the opposition
With delightful unreason
The boys sponsor error
For a brief season—
Though set firm and sure
At the heart's core
Are convictions a philosopher
Might sell his dreams for.
The girls rise quick to crush
The dark conspiracy,
While truth is for the moment
A star caught in a tree.
In the swift sparring of debate
Agile and beautiful,
Logic swings liltingly
As a Broadway musical.
The morrow's crucial game, the cheers,
The rally quite forgot
In this delicious interim
Of shining thought;
While I am left to wonder
How in this brief match
They could parry error
With such dispatch.
Is it alone the magic
Of that Gaelic scholar's skill
Who tutors them in lineage
Of haloed Colmcille?
Or, the not too unlikely

Possibility
That Aquinas tossed them a script
That I did not see?
But I have my answer
Before their words are done—
They have caught this wisdom
From the lips of One
Who taught the young David
To dispose of such rebels
As Goliath, with a sling
And five small pebbles,
God, Who brightens all young things
As their minds unfurl,
And Who told His only Word
To a little girl.

INTERROGATIVE

Who can give answer to your questioning
Why the swift bird should fall with splintered wing?
Or the young child lie
Broken beneath the sky?
Why the first rose should know a blight?
Why in the city of the heart
There is a dreadful night?

Plato sought answers where the shadows run
In a cave pinioned by the sun;
The Stagirite
Teased the tall gates of reason night by night;
While stoics wrestling with inexorable fate
Chide death for being late.

Yet to this mystery
You hold the key.

A bare tree burgeoned on a hill,
Whose branches brushed the sky
High as your Christ was high;
Who, lithe limbs stark to the wood,
Beneath a thorn-thatched hood
Died and did not die—

But lives unendingly
In flesh of your humanity
To raise new calvaries
Over the sin parched sod,
Whereon new Christ's shall hang
Whose bright veins run with God.

This is the simple answer
Even a child may understand
And cup in its small hand,
And yet a mystery still—
Since pain took glory on,
And sorrow bloomed on a hill.

I searched in the shops of song
And the marts of prayer
For a little gift for you,
But none was there

To match the poignant word
I held in my heart;
No text could compass it,
No singer's art.

So without prayer to say
Or song to sing,
Out of my poverty
This simple thing

I give, this little lamp
Troubling the dark,
Christ-lit, and blown to flame
From an infinite spark.

Light it when imminent night
Obscures the town,
When the stars grow restless and wild,
And the winds come down.

Hold it against the dark
Of pain and dread;
It will be peace and light,
And wine and bread.

Some seek a lifetime through
Nor ever find
A lamp that will bravely shine
Through the bitter wind.

A love steadfast as stars,
Gentle as night,
Flooding each aperture
With healing light.

God did not wish the snows
To sweep your sill—
There was a joyous warmth
Within His will

When He set your house on a rock
In a sunlit land,
And a singer at your door
With a lamp in her hand.

TROUBADOUR
(For T.H.)

God set your hand to strong things, poised your spirit
For an upsoaring flight
On lanes of sun past where the last stars singing
Trouble the gates of night.

He placed a seal of the rood on your heart, your forehead,
Tempered its breadth and length;
Against the upthrust of the world's brief beauty
Sinewed your arm with strength.

He laid a song on your lips that he who listens
Might learn this radiant thing—
Within the mansions of God's golden city
All his children sing.

He spilled a wisdom from your pen, with splendor
To light the stumbling mind
Past Plato and the bards to where Truth towers
Gloriously unconfined.

Who lifts your latch and stands a graceless beggar
By some strange hunger stirred,
Receives as alms to fill his empty spirit
Coin of a burning word

That in shadowy shops of pain may win for the asking
A branch from Calvary's tree,
Brighter than Virgil's golden bough, more laden
With immortality.

When I remember you I shall remember
Lilt of a song that tore the darkness through;
From out the templed flesh persistent shining
The One, the Good, the True!

JOAN, BE SWIFT

Joan, be swift at the parapet
There are long, dark shadows beneath the sun;
Snatch your shield from the wall of heaven,
With the grey of ships the waters run.

France is a-quiver with steel and shell
Pas-de-Calais to Brittany;
Rivet your armor and leave the sky
For the chalk cliffs slanting into the sea.

Have you not heard the voices, Joan?
They have pushed the gates of sky apart
And made all heaven lean to hear
The names we name with an anxious heart.

Snatch your sword from its deep-worn sheaf,
The dark foe charges from hill and town;
His breath is flame on the Norman coasts,
Joan, be swift and smite him down.

Girl of the staunch and daring soul,
Stand with our men till the lands are free,
Haunt each lane in the cloud-hung heaven,
Sail each shining strip of sea.

Swear by the cross upon your breast,
Swear by the sword of Roncevalles,
That France shall rise, and peace shall lie
Like sun on the world's wide littoral.

Not with the tight-budded tree outside my window
Does my heart sing,
But with some tangled olive leaning seaward
On the strafed slopes of an Italian spring.

Nor where the crocus braves the latest snowings
Do I take joy

SPRING—1944

While I am hiding in some tropic jungle
Close to some stripling lad, some dreaming boy.

The air is strung with song. I pass unheeding
The lyric symmetries,
For I am with the men on seven oceans
Under the gold tents of the Pleiades.

Spring has me restless, with my spirit soaring,
Leaping the sea's blue line
To rubbled hills where ancient cities smoulder,
And children huddle at a roadside shrine.

I need no compromise with time and distance
To brush the stars with prayer;
Attu, Hollandia, Imphal, Cassino,
God lets me send my spirit anywhere.

Spring never took me with such strength of willing
To make my cry
One with the tears of mankind sorrow-hearted,
Till God's bright bird of peace furrows the sky.

According to a tradition, when St. Peter had escaped from prison and was fleeing from Rome along the Appian Way, he met Christ coming toward him carrying the cross. When Peter asked, "Domine, quo vadis [Master, whither goest thou]?" Christ replied, "I am going to Rome to be crucified again," whereupon Peter repented and returned to the city to suffer martyrdom.

At the first crossroads on the Appian
Taut as a young pine stands
Christ of the wounded feet, the wounded hands.

And none dare ask Him as one Peter did,
"Quo vadis?" knowing well
Up to the gates of heaven, the gates of hell

He goes beside them, in them, over them—
An infinite, lightsome load—
On the roads set with death, on every road.

Christ on the mountains, Christ upon the plain,
Under each pack and gun;
Christ in the midst, and Christ in every one.

When hate lies like a rapier in the waves,
In the blood-churning tide
The eager arms of Christ are open wide.

When wings streak death and hurtle down the sky
Plunging to dark alarms,
Beneath them are the everlasting arms.

Christ in the foxholes, Christ upon the cliffs
Leading the first patrol;
Christ in the frightened heart, and tired soul.

Thabor may be some valley deep with death,
With Christ transfigured still;
And Calvary be any casual hill.

AT THE THIRD MILESTONE

(The Allied armies entering Rome along the Appian Way pass the catacombs of St. Callixtus.)

The dark invader left them unmolested—
What voice can rise from cities of the dead?
The hot shells pound the sea, the sky drops fire,
And men are bled.

These labyrinthine streets are fathoms under
A surf that breaks in larks and blowing wheat;
Hands that are dust can never thrust a weapon
Or force defeat.

But this is living dust! O foe, remember,
These temples were long tenanted by flame;
These are taut branches of a vine whose blooming
Death cannot claim.

They hear young feet upon the ancient highway,
At the third milestone steel wings dark the sun,
Anzio and Sorrento are behind them,
The foe undone.

The tufa tunnels deep beneath the grasses
Are quick with rushing feet upon the floor,
Sixtus, Cornelius, Lawrence, Cecilia
Are at the door

To greet the strong, the brave, the loved forever,
They run with joy to take their tired hands;
On the eternal seacoasts none are strangers;
Nor alien lands.

The centuries have yearned toward this bright morning
When peace shall walk like flame down this old way—
As in God's swift sight two thousand years are reckoned
As a single day!

Where night veers sharply over Kumhwa
Hushing the ridges with soft stars,
And the merciful snow is futile cloak to cover
The wakeful sleepers of yesterday's battle—
Who shall upbraid the heart for questioning
If still there be
In skies, on earth, or in the under-sea
Some power to strike
Love from these ruins and wisdom from disaster?

Along the inscrutable channels of the mind
Let logic lie; there is a swifter knowledge
Straight as the gaze of eagle to the sun!
If you will kneel like a child your love will see
With luminous certainty
What the last little straggling star over Sniper Ridge
Sees this tremendous night:

Lacking decorum of cave, on the windy hillside
A little Hebrew girl walks lissome and lovely
Searching each inch of terrain, while her child
Begotten before the sun and the morning star,
Waits in her delicate doors with divine impatience
His moment of Bethlehem.

From the frozen rocks her feet strike canticles
As she enters each foxhole and lifts each tarpaulin
Seeking the face that you are seeking for.
Her rubric needs no landscape of angel armies,
Nor her strategy savants and diplomats
To plot for peace in some wild speculation,
For this is peace—its presage and definition—
This child she lays within the tired arms
Of the khaki shepherds who watch on Triangle Hill.

For past and future lie in God's hand like music
Resolved in an exquisite now:
And our intricate hour is that far Judean midnight
As love leaps lightly in ten thousand mangers,
Your son, her son, as she takes her place beside him.
This holy night Korea is Bethlehem.

IN SYMBOL AND ANALOGY

BRIGHT STRANGER

With saffron tempora one final stroke
And through the fissured wall the dark withdrew;
I did not know you present till you spoke
Questioning my art, "Is that light breaking through?"
Startled, I answered you with little grace,
Annoyed, that so my solitude was stirred,
Had I but turned and looked into your face
I might have parried with a softer word.
We move in symbol and analogy:
A stranger's casual question thrusts direct
To the mind's core and sets truth running free
Along the rivers of the intellect
To show me what another light was for—
This brightness standing tall within my door.

ON RE-READING A LETTER

These are the lines that wrought the quickening—
Not of the gentle burden of the text,
But the task done, this thought laid like a wing
To shield my littleness; this wisdom flexed
To meet my human need; this glory won
From a small cry that slipped the will's control—
And from a shining field I glean the sun
That opens me a window on your soul.

This the bright ven of fire within the stone,
The rainbow-raveled breast of the grey dove,
In the dark dirge the crystal undertone—
These limpid words you thought so lightly of—
In the stern night have made to wake and start
The miracle child of song within my heart.

THE BIRD

Against the rigors of an austere season
A bird flew into my garden one dark night;
Flung from some mew in the stars, this sweet unreason
Of song cut flaming through the chill and blight.
Such canticle might have leaped in Bernard's mellow
Matins, or shattered silences that stirred
In Juan's stark, mystic cell in Duruelo—
In all my woods there never was this bird.
What can I do to stay this plumed one winging
Into the lonely places where I hide?
I have no defence against his deathless singing
But to kneel at the sill and fling the shutter wide—
Praying that voice to flood each path and glen
That all my garden be made bright again.

THE TRAVELER

I have been searching for some metaphor
For the journeying of the mind toward eternal brightness:
Across two burning strips of desert floor
I know the will parched to an autumn lightness
That the wind could beat to a flame when the night is parted
On quiet acres sown with austerity,
Till love leaps like a young child April-hearted,
Who comes upon bright mountains suddenly.

Though you guard the season well, I still divine it
Through a snare of tensile branch and iron sky;
In futile, empty words I will define it—
The sure and changeless chart you travel by—
A bird winnows your heart with deathless wing,
Whose voice is your sun, your snows, your endless spring.

AGAINST THIS WIND

Why should I cloak you from this withering night
Who am as shelterless as a striken bird?
Or feed you little songs for your delight
Who draw my living from your lightest word?
Proffer my fragile staff to you whose hand
Is strength and sunlight on my splintered sea,
Whose voice if it but whispered on my land
I would come swift as April and as free?
Except that I have read the sky and fear it
May lash a storm about our little town
To twist and bend and break the exquisite spirit
When the tall oaks like brittle reeds go down;
Against this wind that splits the soul apart—
Here are my cloak, my staff, my singing heart!

TALISMAN

We need not speak in symbols any more.
This is the word precise and literal
That translates the bright text across your door,
The talisman that marks this interval.
This is the wood I saw you hang upon—
The two-branched tree that set your body's norm
Taut to its length till you could gaily don
It like a garment and laugh at the storm.

If on this blessed timber you were broken,
It is the human phrase that names it so;
Your spirit straight and integral is spoken
So much by flame, that in each place I go
And feel your shadow falling on my sight,
Quick—I must hide my face against your light.

With this small key I softly shall unlock
The wide rooms of your silences and stand
Clear of the labyrinth of hurt and shock,
Safe in the acres of a speechless land;
Knowing if you but hold me in your thought
I am well housed, if in your inmost heart
You speak my name, I am superbly taught
Though girders of all knowledge break apart.

I had not dreamed that any mortal weather
Would blow me a love as gracious and as wise,
Nor all the larks of April singing together
Match the brave music of your quiet eyes;
Beyond all friends have given of light and grace—
Have I been blessed by looking on your face.